AutoCAD on a Fast Track

A selection of the best tips, recommendations and shortcuts in AutoCAD.

Bonus material: 3D tutorials for architectural design.

Written by an AutoCAD user who has 20 years of professional experience with this software package.

Author: Lars Boye Nielsen

Table of Contents

Prologue

This book is not meant to be a comprehensive book about AutoCAD. It's a book that helps you use AutoCAD in a faster and easier way. Imagine running from start to finish in an orienteering race. You want to get to the finish as fast as possible. Read the map correctly, so you avoid touching the wrong post, Apply what you have been reading, so you can be efficient in your work. Moreover it will bring you more satisfaction in your daily work with AutoCAD.

From 20 years of experience I have gathered valuable tips and shortcuts in AutoCAD. I've seen how wrong you can use the software and how you can use it in a smart and more efficient way. I am convinced that you will benefit from using my tips and recommendations. In the 3D tutorials you get an introduction to some great 3D features in AutoCAD. Notice that the 3D commands only can be used in AutoCAD 2007 and later releases.

As a Mechanical Designer or Architect you want to reach your design goals with ease. I hope you find this guide easy to read and understandable.

Get a Good Start on a Fast Track

Template

Create a template that you use each time you start a new drawing. Start a new drawing and create a template that contains the required layers, custom menus, textstyles, dimstyles, drawing limits and settings in the status bar or settings in the options menu. Use "save as" to save the drawing with the extension "dwt". Now you have saved the drawing as a template. Make sure you have saved the template in the default template folder that is specified in the AutoCAD menu under options - files. This template will save your time, because you don't need to create the settings every time you start a new drawing. AutoCAD will use a default template, if you don't make your own template. But this template contains only a few layers and many settings need to be changed.

Quickly Start a New Drawing

The QNEW command combined with a template can be the fastest way to start a new drawing. When you use the following settings, QNEW immediately starts a new drawing without displaying any dialog boxes or prompts, do the following:

1. In the command line you set the FILEDIA system variable to 1.

2. In the command line you set the STARTUP system variable to 0.

3. Bring Options dialog, switch to Files tab and specify QNEW template in Template Settings, Default Template File Name for QNEW.

Drawing Limits in AutoCAD

The drawing limits are there for a good reason. When you start a new drawing, and then decide how much space you need for the drawing. Think of it as the size of your drawing area. Then you can define drawing limits correctly. Type LIMITS enter. Type 0, 0 as lower left corner then type or click the coordinate for upper right corner. Furthermore, the drawing limits define the extent of ZOOM all. Tip: You can make a little space around the drawing frame, if you define drawing limits a inch outside the drawing frame. This makes it easier to do a PLOT with the option "window".

Disappearing Hatch and Fast Regen

If you open an R12 or earlier drawing in R14 or later, and cannot see the hatching, then you need to check the FILLMODE setting. If FILLMODE is set to OFF, the hatching will not show. This is to speed up REGEN times. Make hatches visible by setting FILLMODE to ON. You type 1 in the command line. Zero will set it to OFF.

Purge

The data from an AutoCAD drawing consumes the resources on an IT system. Therefore you must regularly remove unnecessary data from a drawing. You do this with the PURGE command. In older version before 2000 you have to write PURGE in command line, at the prompt "do you want to purge all objects? Type yes, enter. In newer versions, you use a dialog box, selectively you choose what kind of objects you want to purge. Only use purge when the drawing is complete. Else you might remove layers or text styles that you wanted to keep.

Design Center

I believe the Design Center in AutoCAD is a very useful tool. With Design Center you can find and reuse layers, layouts, linetypes, dim styles, text styles, hatches and blocks from other drawings. Certain parts of a drawing can be copied into another drawing easily. Choose the parts in right side of dialog box. Drag and drop the parts into the drawing area of the DWG file that you have open. Blocks can be categorized and used in the tool palette. Make a library of blocks or hatches in tool palettes. Simply click on a block from Design Center and drag it over to a tool palette, drop it when the cursor is above the gray area of a tool palette. This feature in AutoCAD is great, because it makes your work easier and saves a lot of time!

Tool Palettes

Use the tool palettes as organized menus. Place them on the right side, if you are right-handed. Add your favorite commands, dimstyles, textstyles, hatches, blocks and materials on tool palettes. Organize tool palettes so you can easy view and access your tools. I recommend the following: Move all tool palettes into palette groups. This way the tool palettes are organized and it is easier to find them. Right-click in the bigger gray area on a tool palette, now click **Customize Palettes**. In the left side of dialog box you organize the palettes alphabetic by dragging them up or down. In the dialog box, move all the tool palettes from the left side into palette groups on right side. In the right side of dialog box you organize the palette groups alphabetic by dragging them up or down. Close the dialog box when you have organized the palettes. Again right-click in the bigger gray area on a tool palette. Next click "Sort by Name", this will display the list of tools in alphabetic order. In the same shortcut menu, adjust the size of images and text in "View Options". On the tool palette you can use autohide, if you want more space on the screen. A great feature is that you can create tool palettes with different dynamic blocks. You can add dynamic behavior to existing block libraries. For example you can interactively stretch the block with a list of lengths. Or rotate and move a block with dynamic behavior.

Blocks: I advise that you mainly use blocks in your drawing, they are much easier to move and rotate.

Command Alias

A command alias is an abbreviation that you enter at the command prompt instead of entering the entire command name. You are using commands in AutoCAD all the time; therefore will this practice save you a lot of time. Moreover you will relieve your hand by using it less.

For example, on the keyboard you can enter *a* to start the ARC command. An alias is different from a keyboard shortcut, which is a combination of keystrokes, such as CTRL+N for NEW.

An alias can be defined for any AutoCAD command, device driver command, or external command. The second section of the acad.pgp file defines command aliases. You can change existing aliases or add new ones by editing acad.pgp in an ASCII text editor. To open the PGP file, Click Tools menu - Customize - Edit Program Parameters (acad.pgp). The file can also contain comment lines preceded by a semicolon (;). Before you edit *acad.pgp*, it would be a precaution to create a backup so that you can restore it later, if needed.

To define a command alias, add a line to the command alias section of the *acad.pgp* file using the following syntax:

Abbreviation,*command

Where *abbreviation* is the command alias that you enter at the Command prompt and *command* is the command being abbreviated. You must enter an asterisk (*) before the command name to identify the line as a command alias definition.

If you can enter a command transparently, you can also enter its alias transparently. When you enter the command alias, the full command name is displayed at the Command prompt and the command is executed.

You can create command aliases that include the special hyphen (-) prefix, that accesses a command that displays a command prompt instead of a dialog box. Exclude the prefix (-) and you see a dialog box when you enter the command alias, surely only for those commands where a dialog box is accessible.

BH, *-BHATCH

BD, *-BOUNDARY

Note: It is not recommended to use command aliases in customization files. If you edit *acad.pgp* while AutoCAD is running, enter **REINIT** to use the revised file.

Toolbars and Menus

Place toolbars on the user interface in a location that gives you the shortest distance to move the mouse. Activate only the toolbars and menus that you need for your job. Customize the toolbars with the CUI feature. Include only the commands in the toolbar that are required for your work. Type CUI enter. Now you see the Customize User Interface, here you click 3D modeling (current), next you click Customize Workspace. See image below.

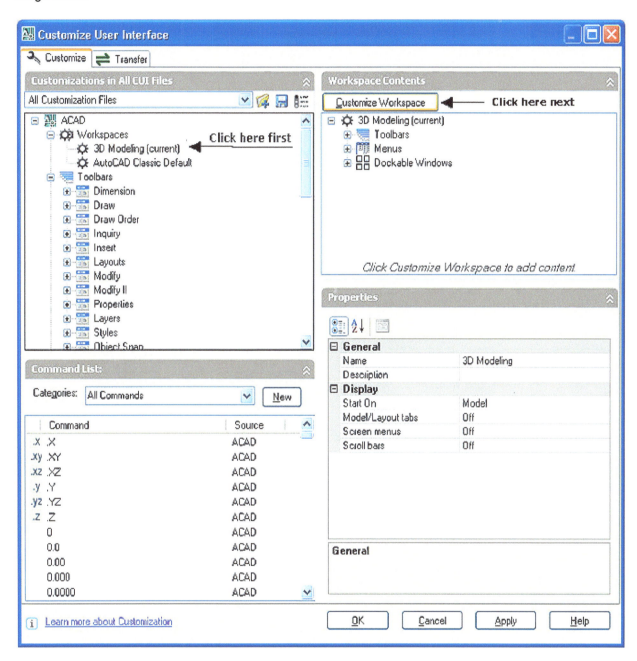

Now open the small boxes by clicking the +. in the upper left side of menu (customization in ALL CUI Files. Add menus and toolbars by clicking the square boxes, a green check will appear. Finally click done in right side of CUI and click OK to apply changes in AutoCAD.

Optimal use of Layers

How can you use the layers in AutoCAD to work more efficient?

Here is a list of things you can do:

1. In the Layer Manager you create layers with proper meaningful names. F. ex. Ground floor, first floor, second floor, third floor etc.

2. Use only layers that are necessary in the drawing. Use the purge command to remove layers.

3. Freeze layers that you are not currently working with. The drawing becomes easier to work with.

4. Use layers, who have different colors assigned. Using different colors can help you distinguish layers in various views.

5. Use the different functions in the layer manager, they are excellent. You can filter out the layers you want to look at. That could be necessary if you have many layers in the drawing.

6. In the Layer Manager you can organize the layers in groups. One group for ground floor, another group for first floor etc. It's a good idea in bigger projects. Select **New Group Filter** in Layer Manager. Next add layers to your group filter from the drawing.

7. To create a continuous revision of your drawing, create a separate layer for notes and labels that explain the drawing and what still needs to be done or corrected. Freeze this layer when the drawing is completed.

Tips for 2D Drafting

Grips to Edit 2D Objects

1. Select the objects to copy.

2. Select a base grip on a 2D object by clicking the grip. The selected grip is highlighted (turns red), and the default grip mode, Stretch, is active.

3. Cycle through the grip modes by pressing ENTER until the grip mode you want appears (stretch, move, rotate, or scale). Choose rotate.

4. Next choose a basepoint.

5. Enter *C* (Copy).

6. Now you can make copies of your object, for example around a circle, by pointing some angles with polar tracking. Copies continue being made until you turn off grips.

7. Turn off grips by pressing SPACEBAR or ESC.

Speed Up the Erase Command

Execute the command CUI. Under toolbars – modify you find the erase command, next look at properties. The Macro command line should read - ^C^C_erase. Change this line to read - *^C^C_erase single. So when you erase objects, just click on them and they will disappear at once. You don't need to confirm each selection with the right mouse button. You can apply this little coding trick to all the editing commands. I think it's a great way to speed up your work.

Object Fields

It is easy to create object fields that are located in the same space as the object to which they are associated, what about if the object is located in modelspace, but you want the field to be displayed in the layout? You can do this very easily by starting to create the field in the same space as the object. Before you exit the field dialog box, highlight the Field Expression at the bottom of the dialog box. Next you right-click and choose Copy. Cancel the dialog box and then switch to the layout. Right-click and choose paste to create a Mtext object with the field data. Additionally you can also paste the code into a table cell.

Rotate Coordinate System and Draw in an Angle

You can create portions of a drawing at an angle. This is how you do it: Rotate the User Coordinate System around the Z-axis to the angle. You can then use Object Snap Tracking, Ortho, Grid, and Snap relative to the angle.

A Fast Way to Make a Floor Plan in 3D

A fast method to make a drawing such as a floor plan is to use the POLYSOLID command. This command can easily create walls in 3D. First you create the floor with a region that is later extruded with the required height. Next start the POLYSOLID command and type J (justify). Then choose L and snap all 4 corners of the floor. End the command by typing C and pressing enter. Continue creating the remaining walls with polysolid. In the command polysolid you can type W to change width on the walls.

Copy with a Base Point

When you want to copy objects, simply use "COPY TO CLIPBOARD", instead of using the command "COPY WITH A BASE POINT". It lets you pick a base point on the DWG to copy from. Then the basepoint will be used as an insertion point, when you insert a selection of objects. The advantage is that you can specify the exact position in a new drawing window. Useful feature if you want to copy parts of a drawing to another drawing. Try also creating a tool bar button for the command.

Scale with Reference

You probably received a drawing that was scaled wrong. I recommend using this method to change the drawing into a correct scale. To solve the problem use the SCALE command. The procedure is explained here.

Type scale and press enter.

1. First select the objects that you want to scale.

2. Select a basepoint, choose lower left corner.

3. Select Reference and press enter.

4. Select 2 points that defines the total length of the object.

5. Now enter the correct length.

Moving an Object to a Absolute Coordinate

From AutoCAD 2006 Autodesk introduced dynamic input, this displays your coordinates and angle input on-screen in small boxes. The standard setting for this feature creates a little problem, when you type absolute coordinates. The solution is to switch off dynamic input, before you type the coordinates. Just press F12 and you can type the coordinates in the command line.

Draw a 45 degree Angle Arc Counter-Clockwise

Ever get frustrated trying to draw an arc the default counter-clockwise? Try this to draw an arc using "end-end-center". With polar tracking on, draw a 45 degrees "V" shape using equal line segments. Now draw the arc using the right point A of the V as the start point, the left point B of the V as second point and finally the lowest vertex as the center to complete the arc. NB: The UCS must be set to default "world".

Image 1.A

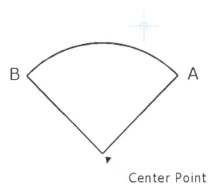

Center Point

Spacetrans

Modelspace viewports in layouts are usually scaled at other than 1:1 ratios. This means that text objects in the viewport may appear at a different size than on the layout, even if they have the same height property. The SPACETRANS command changes distances (typically text heights) from either modelspace or paperspace to an equivalent distance in the other space. This command can be invoked transparently to provide correct values when distances are requested by other commands. If used in standalone mode, this command displays the computed value on the command line.

Scrolling through Directories Searching for Drawings?

In AutoCAD you can add your most frequently used directories in the Open dialog box. Right-click on the far left of the dialog box to add and remove directories.

Trim and Extend

From AutoCAD 2006 a new feature in AutoCAD has appeared. In the TRIM command you can switch to extend by holding down SHIFT, you select the objects first and then press down shift while you click on the end of a line you want to extend. You can do the same with EXTEND command, switch to TRIM. But there is more functionality in these 2 commands. Especially the options Fence and Edge are worth mentioning. With fence at hand you can easily trim or extend multiple lines by making a long cutting line in 2 clicks! The other option I should mention is Edge. With Edge you can extend to an invisible boundary.

Create a line to make an invisible extension. Select the option **Edge** in the Extend command. When AutoCAD prompt; "Enter an implied edge extension mode [Extend/No extend] <No extend>:" Type **E** enter. Next pick a line to create an extension. Imagine the line as a boundary for your extension.

The Better Alternative to Explode

XPLODE is a very good command that allows you to control the color, layer, lineweight and linetype in all the components of an exploded object. It works similarly to EXPLODE, but with more functionality. For example, a block is a compound object. You can explode multiple compound objects simultaneously. Furthermore, it's possible to change the color, layer, lineweight, and linetype of each object individually or change the entire selection set globally. You can specify a color, layer, lineweight, and linetype, or these properties can be inherited from the object being exploded. A compound object contains multiple AutoCAD objects. Xplode breaks a compound object into its component objects.

Can't Find an Object

Use ZOOM extent to find objects that are located far away, outside drawing limits. Always locate objects inside the drawings limits, hence you avoid this problem. In the PROPERTIES command you can also find and select objects by using Quick Select.

Drawing Lines

TIP 1: Use ORTHO to keep your lines at a set angle, for example 90 degrees. Press F8 to turn ORTHO on or OFF. Or press SHIFT to activate or deactivate to ORTHO command.

TIP 2: For odd angles, change polar angle settings (Polar Tracking).

Drawing Rectangles

To draw an exact rectangle, first select a starting point. Type D for dimensions, next type length and width. Move mouse to left or right and left-click, thereby placing the rectangle.

Peditaccept

Formerly in older AutoCAD releases, when you used POLYLINE edit to join a line or arc with other objects, you were prompted to enter Y (for Yes) if you wanted to convert the line or arc into a polyline. By setting the PEDITACCEPT system variable to 1, you can avoid this prompt and proceed directly to joining your line or arc with other objects.

Linear Dimensions by Selection

Want to make a quick dimension? This can be done easily by doing a return, when AutoCAD prompts you for the <First extension line origin>. At this point AutoCAD will ask you to select the line to be dimensioned. Just select a line and place the dimension in a desired location.

Convert Lines to Polylines

From AutoCAD 2006 you can use PEDIT to convert multiple lines or arcs to polylines in one session. This option will save you a lot of time, if there is many lines in the drawing that needs to be converted.

Type PEDIT and press enter. Type M for multiple; choose the lines you want to convert. To the prompt: <Convert Lines and Arcs to Polylines [Yes/No]?> Answer Yes, press enter twice to end command. Or close an open polyline, this is recommendable, because you then only have to move 1 unit. I've used the PEDIT command often; it is a very good tool for modifying polylines.

Creating Polylines of any Closed Space with a Single Click

To create a closed polyline of lines in a closed space, use the BPOLY command (Boundary Command). This command works similar to the hatch command, but creates a closed polyline instead of hatch. Click button Pick Points and click inside a rectangle of lines.

Image 2.A

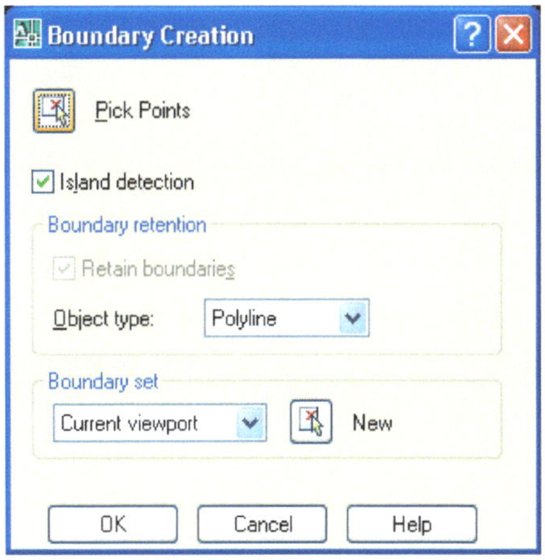

Fence

When you want to cut away multiple lines or circles, then use the sub command fence. The command is versatile with cross-polygon function. The fence sub command can be very time saving when a complex design with many objects needs to be trimmed. The sub command can be used with TRIM and EXTEND command.

Mirror

Use MIRROR command as much as possible. Plan where you want the mirror axis before using the command. Use ORTHO and snap endpoints on mirror axis.

Make a corner

If lines are intersecting at the corner, then you can cut the lines neatly, so you create a corner. Set radius to 0 in FILLET command and click on the 2 lines that are pointing away from the box.

Image 3.A

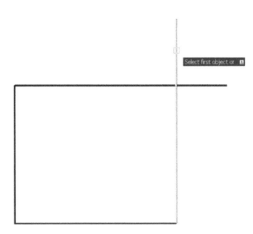

Lengthen an Arc or a Line

Draw an arc with given radius of any length. Then to set its length use the LENGTHEN command with the total option. Type the total distance. Or change the length with the PROPERTIES command. The dynamic option is great if you want to extend an arc or a line from one point to another.

Stretch Command

I find the STRETCH command to be very useful, when you edit objects. With this command it is easy to change the dimensions of multiple lines, a rectangle or triangle. Use a crossing polygon by typing CP to select multiple objects and then stretch them to a desired location. When specifying second point: I move the mouse in the desired direction, then type the distance and press enter. Remember, ORTHO must be on. If you want to do a diagonal stretch, then use Polar Tracking. Procedure: Press F10, and then right click on Polar Tracking in the status bar, next click "settings". Set increment angle to a specific angle. Now do the STRETCH command as described above. NB: In irregular shaped areas use stretch together with subcommand CP (Crossing Polygon).

Circular Viewport

Let's say you want to create a circular viewport. You don't want objects displayed outside the circular viewport, only on the inside of the circular viewport.

Here is what you can do:

1. In a layout viewport, create a circle.

2. Change the circle into a region with the REGION command.

3. Enter the MVIEW command and specify the Object option. Select the circular region. Now you have changed it into a viewport.

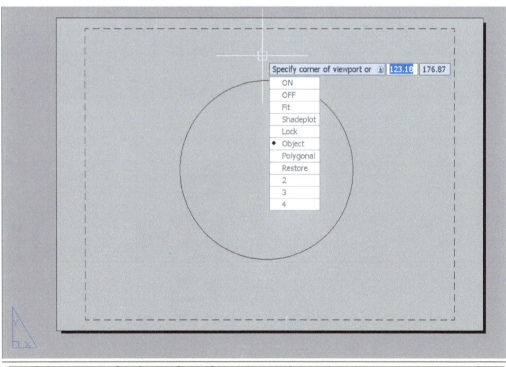

```
Specify base point or [Displacement] <Displacement>: Specify second point or
<use first point as displacement>:
Command: MVIEW
Specify corner of viewport or [ON/OFF/Fit/Shadeplot/Lock/Object/Polygonal/Restore/2/3/4] <Fit>:
123.18, 176.87, 0.00    SNAP GRID ORTHO POLAR OSNAP OTRACK DUCS DYN LWT
```

Restore Viewport Settings with a Click of a Button

While creating a layout, did you ever want to make a change to your model without having to switch to model space? You started to make such a change, only to mess up the scale and limits of your viewport. Fortunately, you can edit your models within paperspace viewports safely with the command VPMAX. In a layout with the desired viewport selected, click on the Maximize Viewport button at the bottom of the AutoCAD screen in the tools tray. Your viewport will switch to model space and expand to fill the AutoCAD screen. You can now safely zoom, edit and pan without fear of ruin the scale and limits in your viewport. When you're done editing, simply press the **Maximize Viewport** button again. You're now back in paperspace and all of your viewport settings are restored to normal. You find the Maximize Viewport Button on the status bar.

Image 4.A

Image 4.B

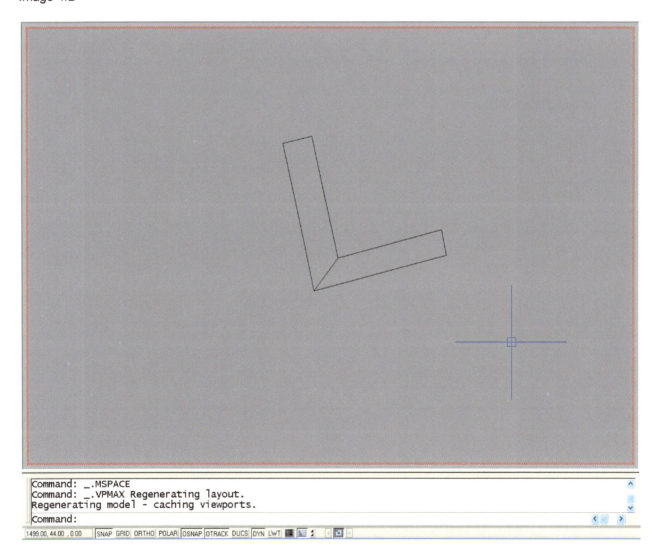

Precision in AutoCAD

SNAP

The SNAP command makes it possible to draft precisely, when you are making a drawing in AutoCAD. Type SNAP enter. Now type 1 or you could type with decimals 0.1 Make a snap setting that is appropriate to the object's size. The result of using SNAP is that your drawing contain objects that are located in coordinates with rounded digits. F. ex. 200. 50, 200.00. I believe most people prefer precise and rounded coordinates. Use OBJECT SNAP, OBJECT SNAP TRACKING and SNAP as much as possible to create accurate drawings.

Object Snap

Always use object snap when you make a drawing. Turn on the object snaps that are necessary for griping the desired points on your drawing object. If you turn on to many object snaps, then you give AutoCAD a hard time choosing the correct point.

Object Snap Tracking

Use object snap tracking to track along alignment paths that are based on object snap points. Acquired points display a small plus sign (+), and you can acquire up to seven tracking points at a time. After you acquire a point, horizontal, vertical, or polar alignment paths relative to the point are displayed as you move the cursor over their drawing paths. For example, you can select a point along a path based on an object endpoint or midpoint or an intersection between objects. In the following illustration, the Endpoint object snap is on. You start a line by clicking its start point (1), move the cursor over another line's endpoint (2) to acquire it, and then move the cursor along the horizontal alignment path to locate the endpoint you want for the line you are drawing (3).

Image 5.A

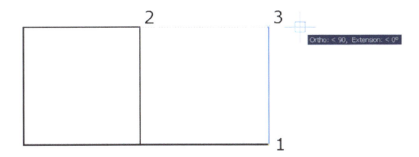

Quick Precise Projections

Use the RAY command instead of XLINE command. Besides creating basic construction lines, it also will create lines at precise angles fast and easy. Use the RAY command with osnap "on" when you make your projections. After trimming, the ray lines become lines. The RAY command never extends the line in 2 directions. The line is extended infinite, but only in one direction from the start point. Advantage: Not wasting time cutting construction lines at both ends. It will save you time, once you get used to the command. CONSTRUCTION LINE command extends the line in 2 directions.

Projection Line from a Circle

Let's say you want to align a projection line from a circle. Pick the RAY command in the draw menu. When asked for start point; press shift on keyboard and simultaneously right click with mouse. Choose Quadrant and start RAY from there in a 90 degree angle. I recommend that you use the RAY command to create projection lines from your drawing objects.

Image 6.A

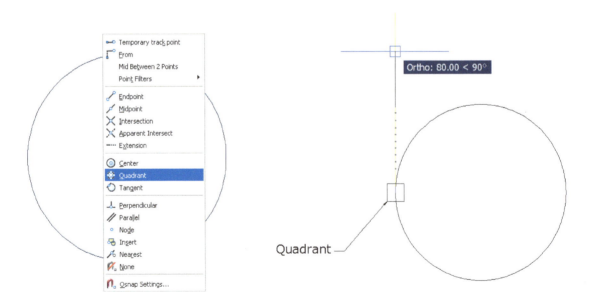

How to Align Text with a Line

Start the session by specifying first source point. See image below.

Image 7.A

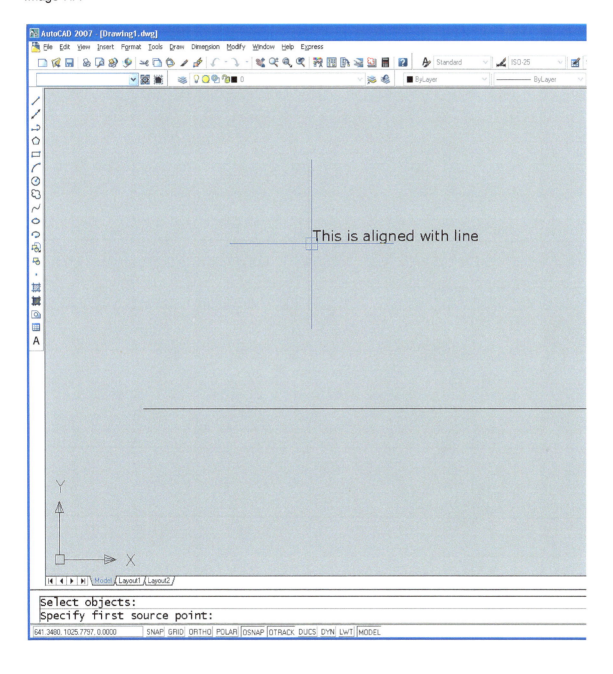

Next you specify first destination point and press enter.

Image 7.B

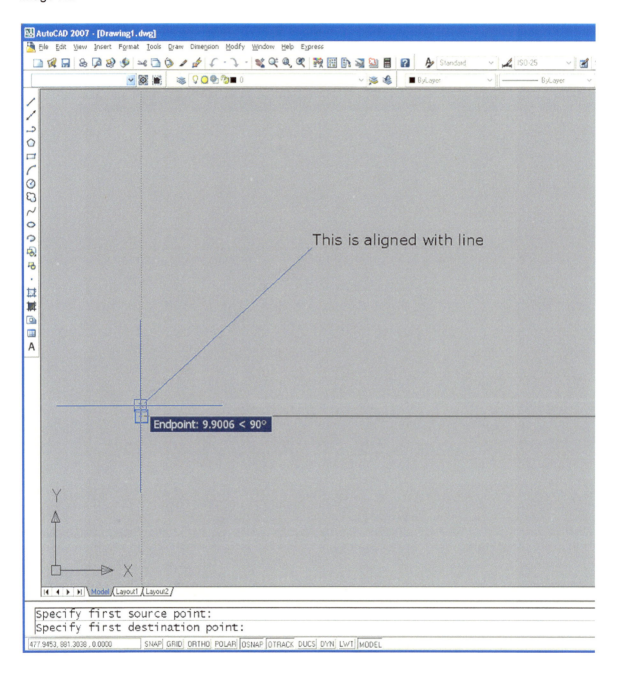

Final result, your text is neatly placed above line.

Image 7.C

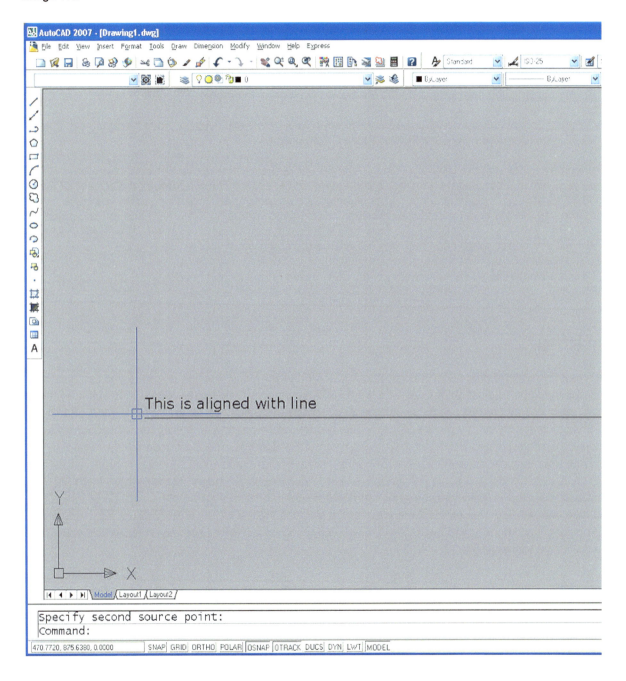

Tips for 3D Rendering, Performance and Modeling

Creating 3D wireframe models can be more challenging than creating 2D drawings. Here are some advices that will help you work more effectively:

1. Create sufficient layers to organize your design. Turn off layers that you currently are not working with. That way you reduce the visual complexity of the model.

2. Create construction geometry to define the basic envelope of the model. See how to do in 3D tutorials.

3. Create and use multiple views, especially isometric views. You will discover that it becomes easier to do 3D modeling, because you see all the sides of an object.

4. Become familiar with the User Coordinate System - UCS. Learn how to make the XY plane in UCS parallel with another plane. Learn that Z is the depth in 3D space. The *XY* plane of the current UCS operates as a work plane to orient planar objects such as rectangles, circles and arcs. The UCS determines the plane of operation for moving, trimming and extending, offsetting, and rotating objects.

5. Always use object snaps and snap, this will ensure the precision of your model.

6. Use coordinate filters to easily locate points in 3D based on the location of points on other objects.

3D Rendering

To save time only render a preview in smaller output size 640 X 480. When making previews you can also use "render cropped region". Adjust output size with the RPREF command. Only use shadows, in final render. Use ray-traced reflections and refractions, when it is needed, namely in scenes with water, marble, glass and mirrors. Shadow mapping display more soft edges and require less rendering time. Ray-traced shadows have more accurate and hard edges, therefore they give a more realistic image. The ray-traced shadows also transmit color from transparent and translucent objects. However this shadow setting requires more rendering time. Often you only need 1 or 2 lights in a smaller scene. The exception is indoor interior, where there are many lamps and spotlights. Only use sunlight in an outdoor scene. If using sunlight, then adjust light intensity, time and date depending on the atmosphere you want to set. Use the necessary time to adjust falloff angle in cone of spotlight, light intensity and the angle from light source to target. Some scenery requires that you combine point light with spotlight.

3D Performance, Optimal Settings for 3D Graphics

Type OPTIONS enter, click on System, and then click on **Performance Settings**. Click on the small "check box" **Adaptive degradation,** so that it's ON. Next "check" all items below. In the dialog box "Adaptive Degradation and Performance Tuning" click Manual Tune. Next "check" to enable **hardware acceleration** and reset to recommended values, continue clicking OK, until you have exited all dialog boxes. Now your graphic should work perfectly with AutoCAD. I know many don't make these settings correct and gets into trouble.

Benefits of using 3D Solids

There are certain benefits when you use 3D solids. From 3D solids you can read mass, volume, centroid, moments of inertia and products of inertia with the MASSPROP command. This information is not possible to get with a box build with surfaces. The exceptions here are regions. From these you can read area, centroid, moments of inertia and product of inertia. And it's easy to edit a solid with grips. Moreover, you can easily create holes, fillets and chamfers on 3D solids. Additionally, you can use Boolean operations on solids, like intersect, subtract and union. My advice: Always use 3D solids or regions, when it's possible in AutoCAD. In architectural design, use region for the floor. Because it's easier to read an area with the MASSPROP command.

Grips for 3D

From AutoCAD 2007 it became possible to use special grips on 3D models. I believe you find these grips very useful when changing the dimension of a 3D object. Activate the grips by pressing down CTRL and clicking on the side you want to move; now you see a blue solid dot. Click on it so it turns red and move the face to a desired location. Be aware that there are 2 different grips for 3D. The other type of grip is for relocating an edge. This grip has a shape as a rectangle, but the procedure is the same.

3D Polyline

A 3D POLYLINE accepts 3D coordinates. When you draw a 3D POLYLINE you are not locked with only X and Y, if you snap to a endpoint. You can specify the coordinates, whether absolute or relative. With 3D POLYLINE you work freely in a 3D space. Hence I prefer to use 3D POLYLINE for 3D modeling.

Invisible edges on 3D faces

When you do more complex 3D modeling it can become necessary to make an edge invisible. You can do this in properties (CTRL+1). Open the properties dialog box. Select a face, then click on "visible" and choose "hidden" for the edge that you want to make invisible.

Shortcut to free 3D Orbit

If you want fast access to the 3DORBIT command, press SHIFT + the middle mouse button. Right-click to display the shortcut menu, this menu has brilliant options.

Control the Smoothness of 3D Objects

If you want to make 3D objects smoother in AutoCAD, then use the FACETRES system variable. With facetres you control the mesh density, which affects the smoothness of 3D surfaces. A higher setting makes the object smoother. I recommend the values 8 - 10. Be aware of more rendering time.

With the VIEWRES command you control the smoothness of curved 2D objects, like circles and arcs. A higher setting in AutoCAD adds more smoothness to the object, I recommend the value 2000.

Select Faces behind on 3D Solids

In AutoCAD 2007 and later 2008 it is possible to select the face behind. For example on a 3D box that would be the face on the backside. Procedure: Place the pickbox on the front face, next press down CTRL, while pressing down CTRL you hit the spacebar once and you see that the face on the back side is selected. Don't click on any faces before AutoCAD has selected the face. It's essential that you place the pickbox virtually on the face behind before you hit the spacebar, see image below. You can also select the other faces using the same procedure.

Image 8.A

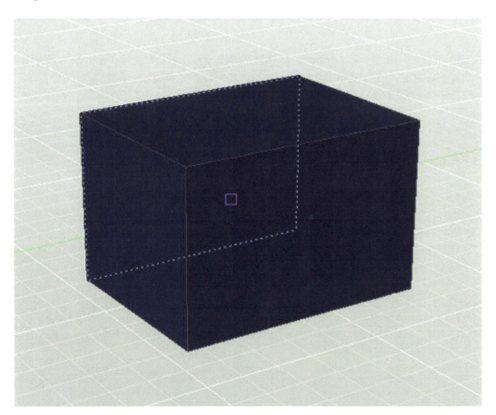

3D Tutorials for Architectural Design

3D Modeling in AutoCAD with Loft Command

With the LOFT command, you can create a new solid or surface by specifying a series of cross sections. The cross sections define the profile (shape) of the resulting solid or surface. It is recommended to use <cross sections only> or "Path", because it's easier to apply than "Guides". Use cross sections with arcs, polylines, lines or polygons. If you use closed polylines or circles as cross sections, then LOFT creates a solid in the space between the cross sections. You must specify at least two cross sections when you use the LOFT command. Use multiple arcs, splines, polylines or lines, if you like to create a open surface. Later, if you want to convert a 3D solid to a surface, then use the EXPLODE command.

First you create 3 splines, next you select them as cross-sections in order from A to C. See image below.

Image 9.A

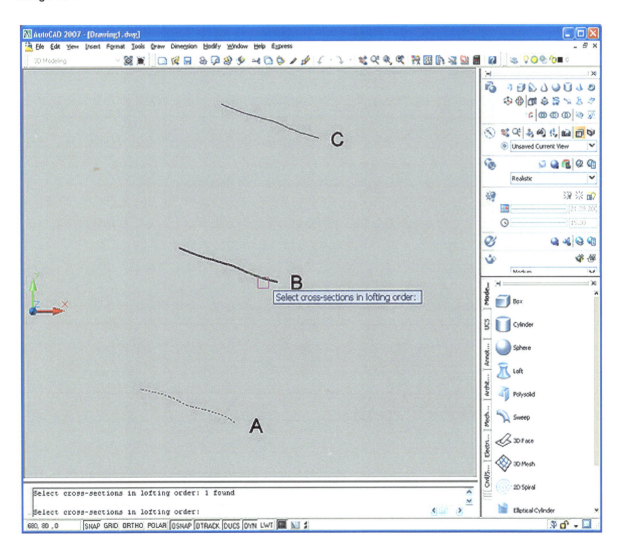

Then you select **cross-sections only**

Image 9.B

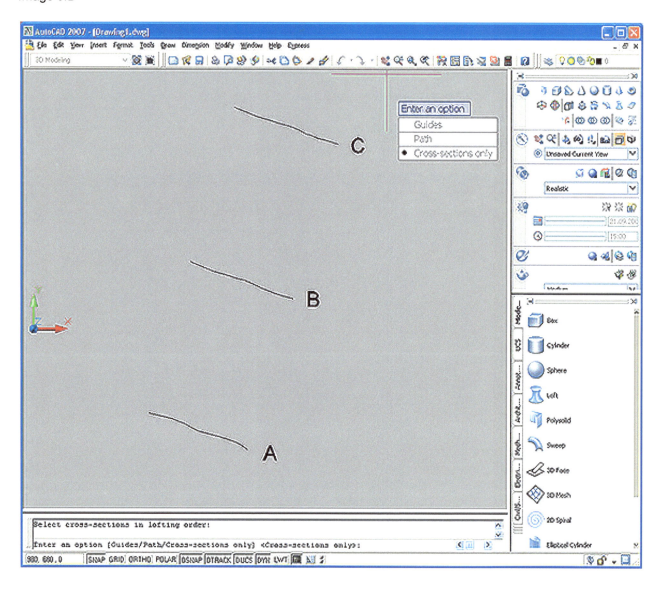

Finally you select **smooth fit** and click ok.

Image 9.C

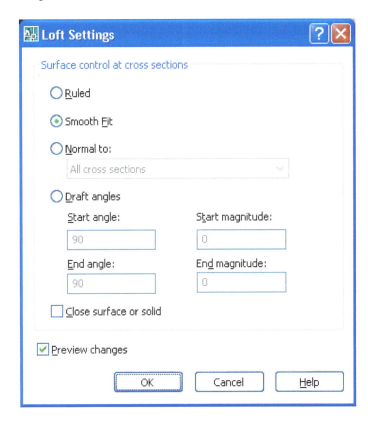

The open surface is created.

Image 9.D

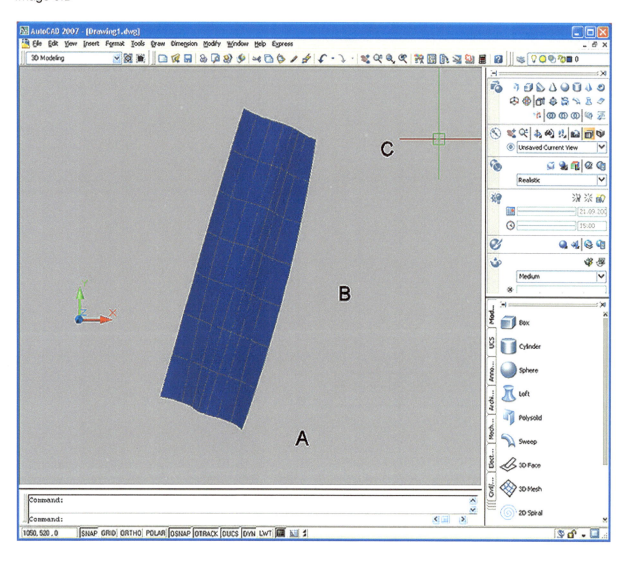

Create a 3D door quickly

With a closed POLYLINE and EXTRUDE command you can quickly create a 3D door.

First draw the door with a polyline as shown on image below.

10.A

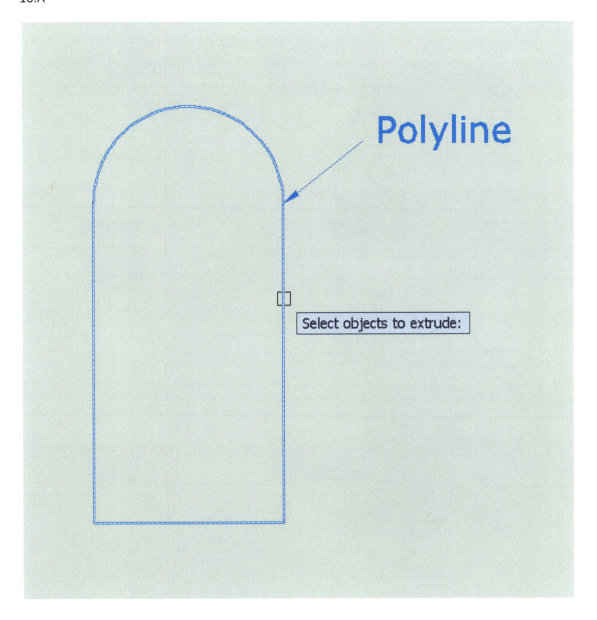

Start the EXTRUDE command. Next select the polyline and specify the desired height, finally press enter.

Image 10.B

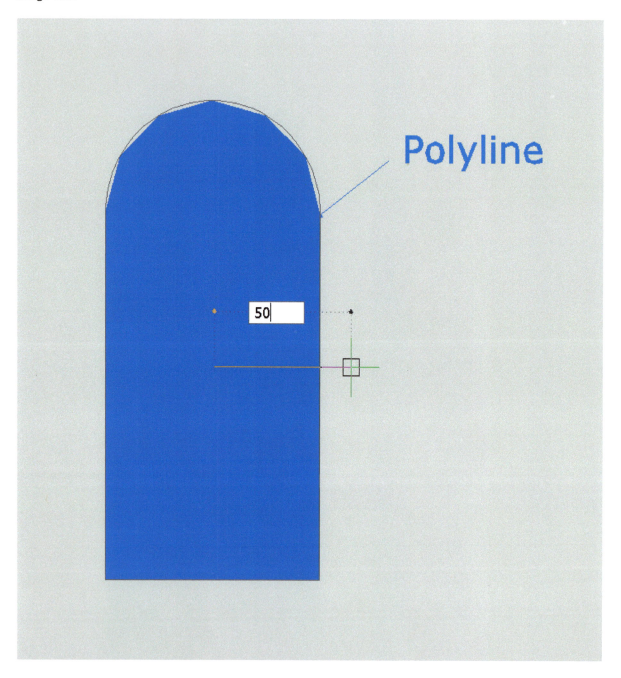

Final result. You created a door in 3D.

Image 10.C

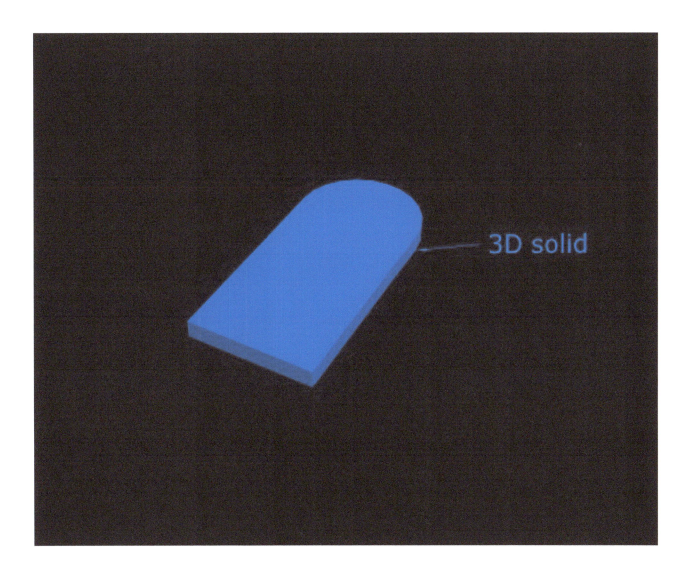

Presspull Command

From AutoCAD 2007 a brilliant new 3D command arrived. It's called PRESSPULL. If you have made a 3D box and want to make a hole through you can do that with the PRESSPULL command. First you create a rectangle with a polyline on top of 1 face on the 3D box. Next you activate PRESSPULL command and click inside the rectangle. Now you can make a hole by pulling the face on the rectangle inside the box. You can use this command for the existing faces of an object, or by imprinting additional faces on an object and pulling those inside or outside. If you pull it outside of the box, then you create a solid object pointing out from the 3D box. You can also use 3D POLYLINE instead of polyline. First align UCS so it's parallel with the side you are making a hole. In the following tutorial I show you how to use the PRESSPULL and the POLYSOLID command.

Creating a Wall with the Polysolid Command

A new 3D command in AutoCAD 2007 was POLYSOLID. Next I show how you create a wall, with a hole for a window. Type polysolid in the command line and press enter. Then type W to specify the width of the wall.

Image 11.A

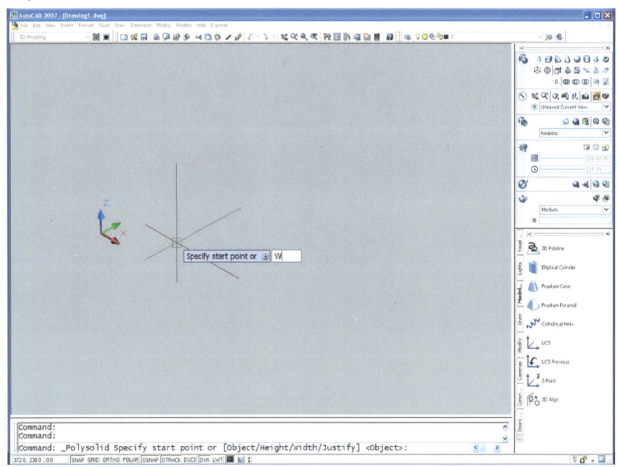

Next you type H to specify the height.

Image 11.B

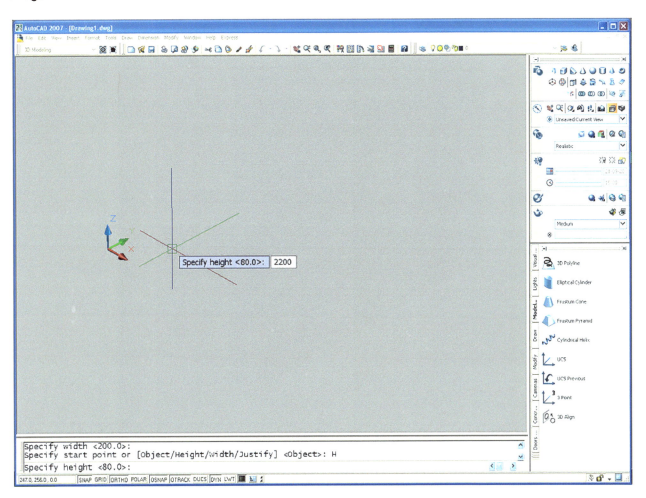

Now you can specify a start point. Move the mouse to the right and type the length of the wall, followed by enter.

Image 11.C

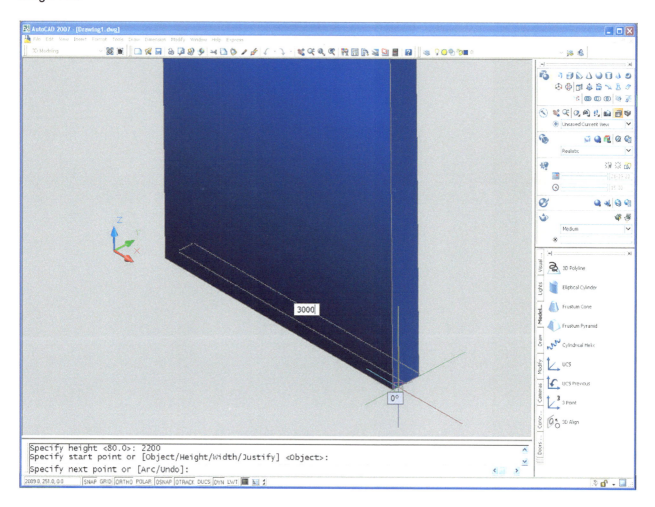

The wall is created.

Image 11.D

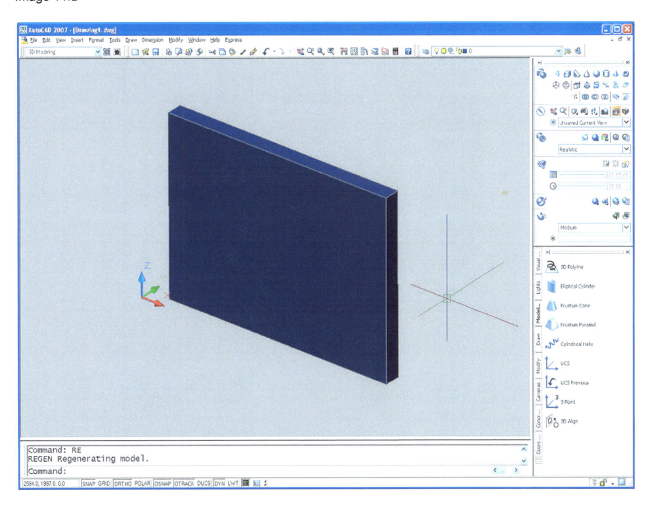

Now you create an opening in the wall. First activate DYNAMIC UCS and OBJECT SNAP.

Image 11.E

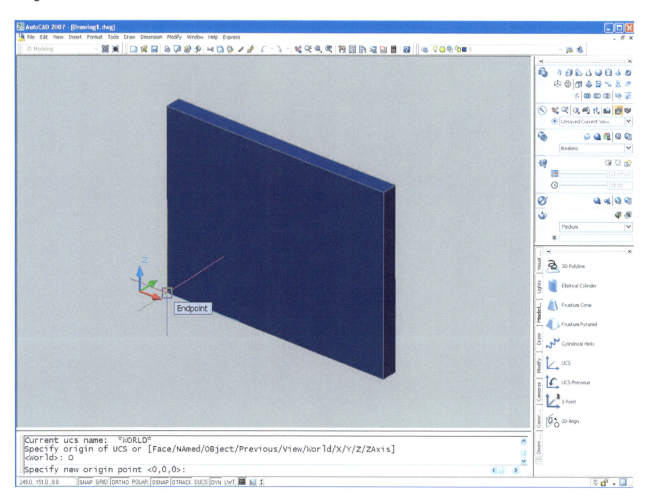

Activate object snap midpoint and object snap tracking. Next start the 3DPOLY command. Snap the middle of the wall's length (without clicking). To specify the start point, you move the mouse to the left and type the distance 450. Execute the command by pressing enter.

Image 11.F

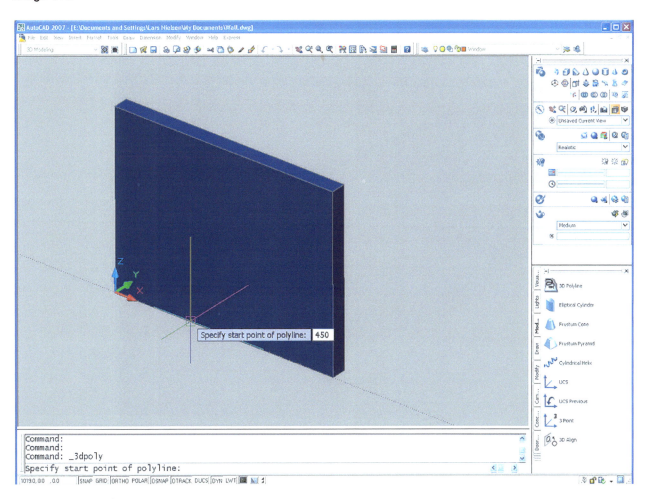

Move the mouse upwards and type the height of the opening, followed by enter.

Image 11.G

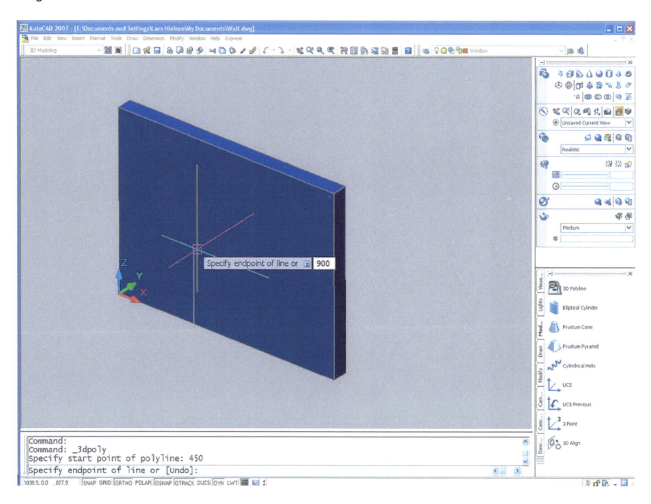

Move the mouse to the right and type the length of the opening, followed by enter.

Image 11.H

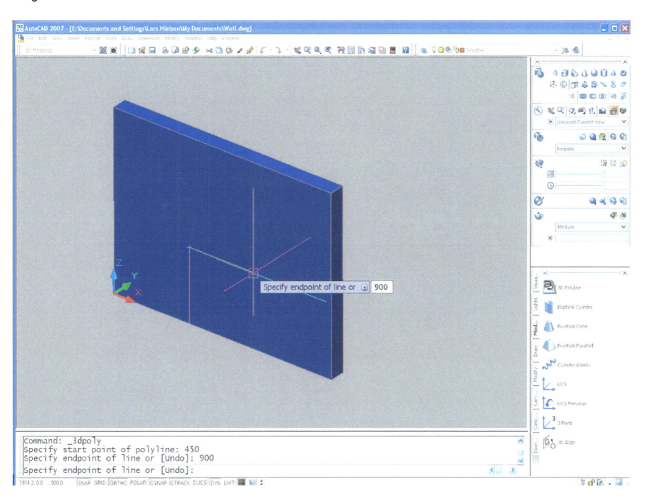

Next you move the mouse down and type the height of the opening.

Image 11.I

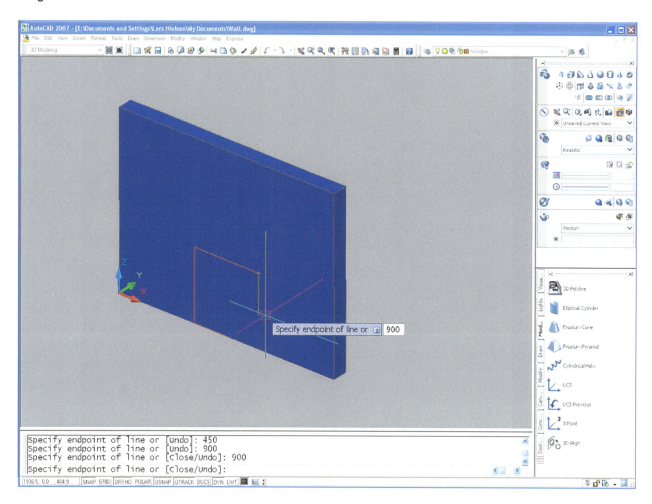

Next you type C to close the 3D polyline.

Image 11.J

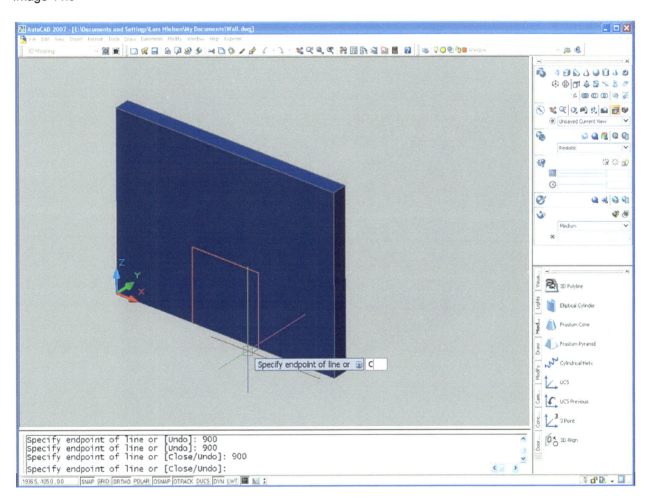

Next you move the window 850 upwards, in an angle of 90 degrees. You have now positioned the window.

Image 11.K

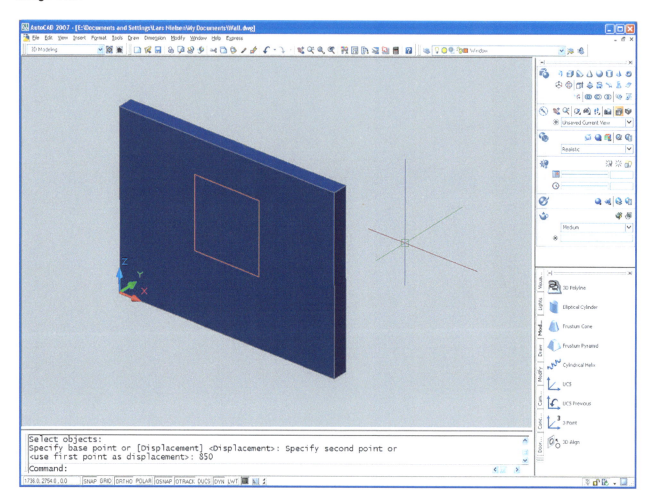

Start the PRESSPULL command in the dashboard and click inside the square.

Image 11.L

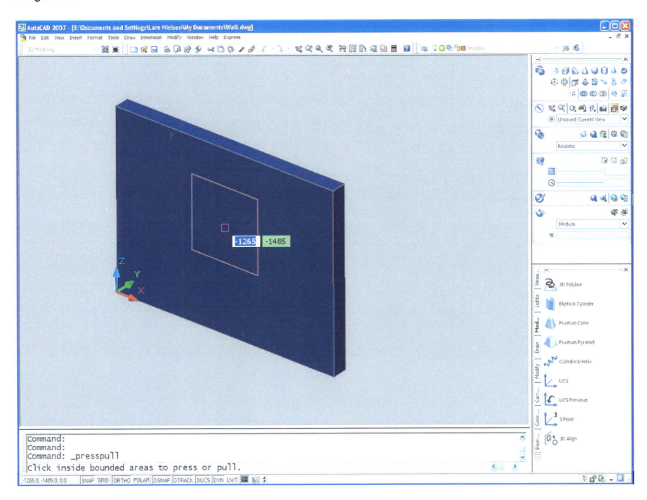

Pull the mouse to the rear and type 500, followed by enter.

Image 11.M

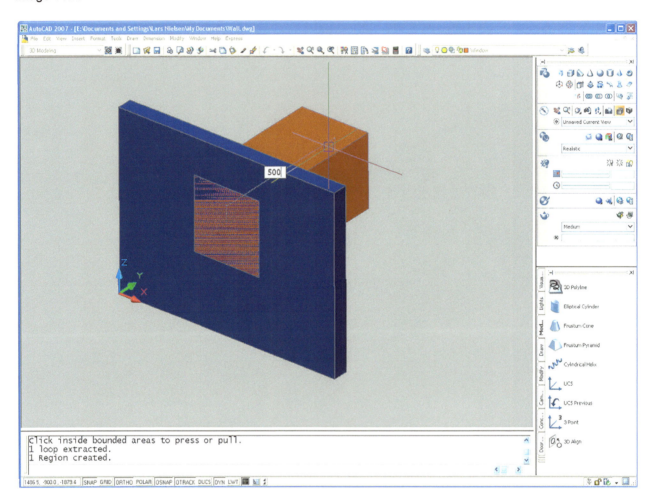

Final result. You created a hole for a window in the wall. You got the job done fairly easy.

Image 11.N

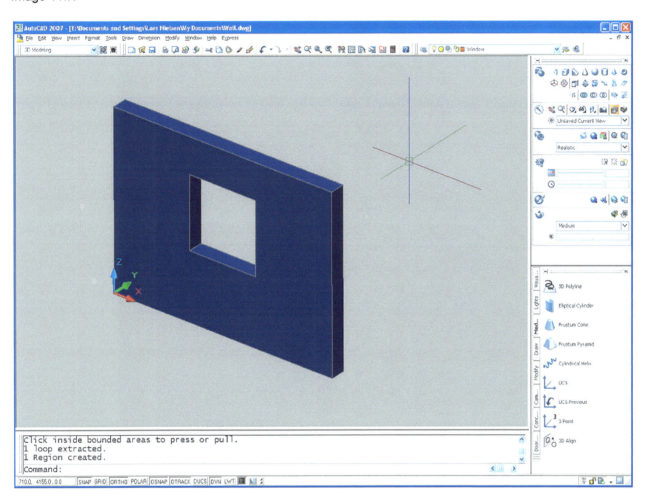

Create a Window Frame with the Sweep Command

Start the task by changing the UCS. Rotate X axis 90 degrees.

Image 13.A

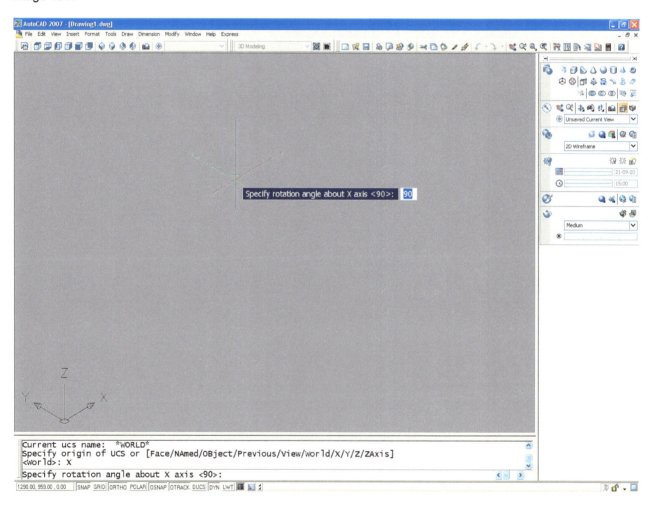

Next you draw a profile of your window frame. In the SWEEP command you need a sweep path; therefore you also draw a rectangle that defines the size of your window frame. In 3D space you place the 2 objects in a 90 degree angle, see image below.

Image 13.B

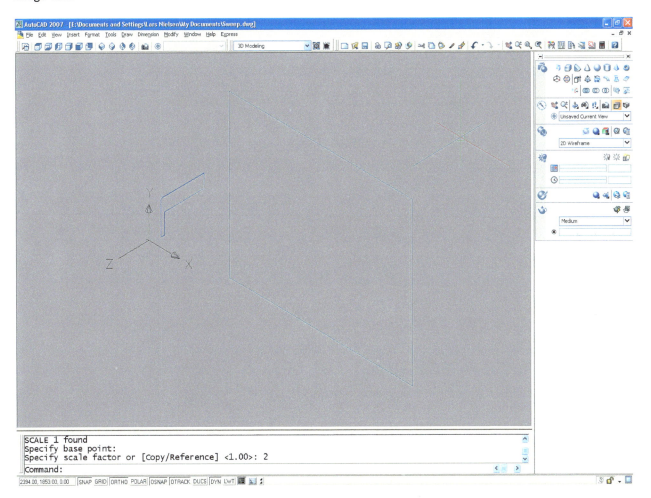

Start the SWEEP command. Now you select the profile as shown on image 13.C

Image 13.C

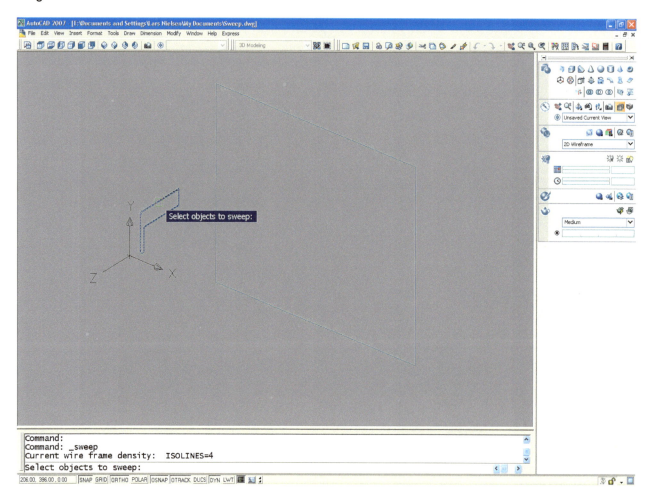

Finally you select the sweep path and press enter.

Image 13.D

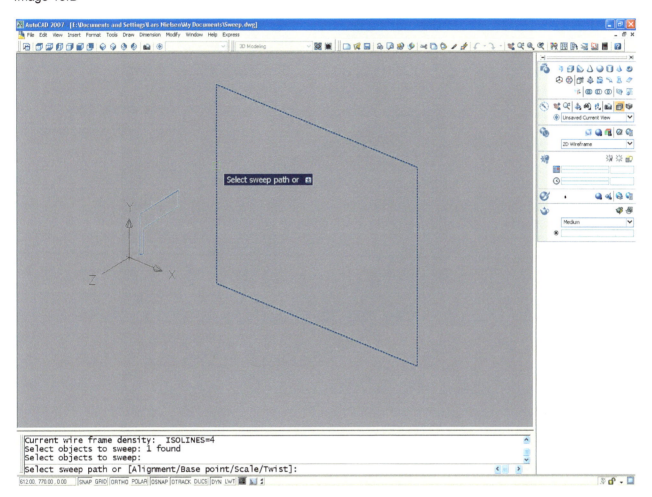

Here you see the result as an image with shades.

Image 13.E

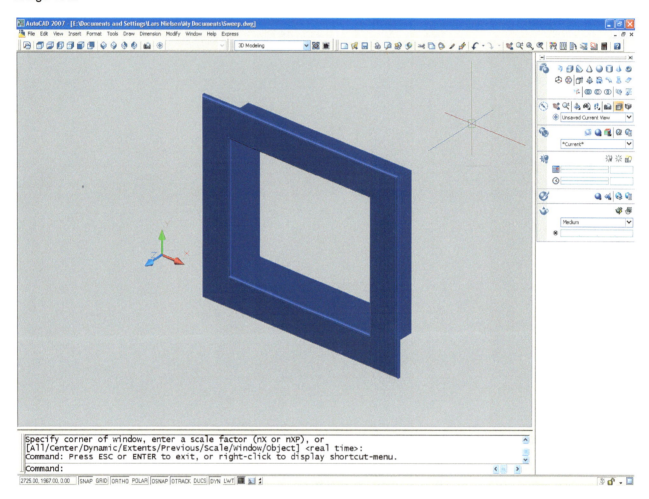

3D Alignment

Another great command is 3DALIGN. With this command you can align an object with other objects in a 3D space. Basically you change their 3D orientation. Here is how you use the command 3DALIGN.

Type 3dalign in the command line. Specify a base point on the corner of the 3D box. See image below.

Image 12.A

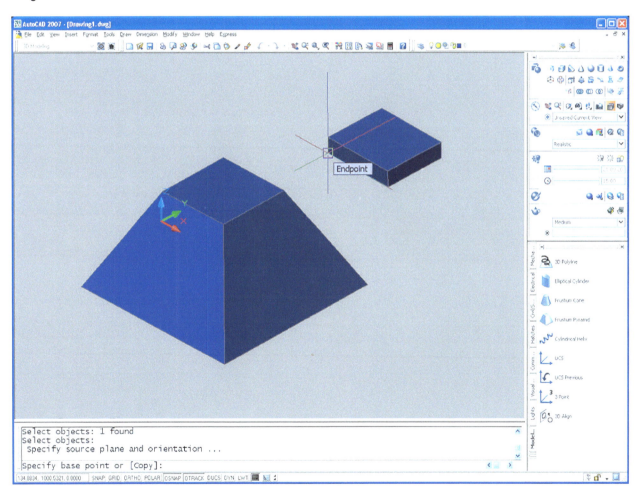

Specify second point as I've shown on image below.

Image 12.B

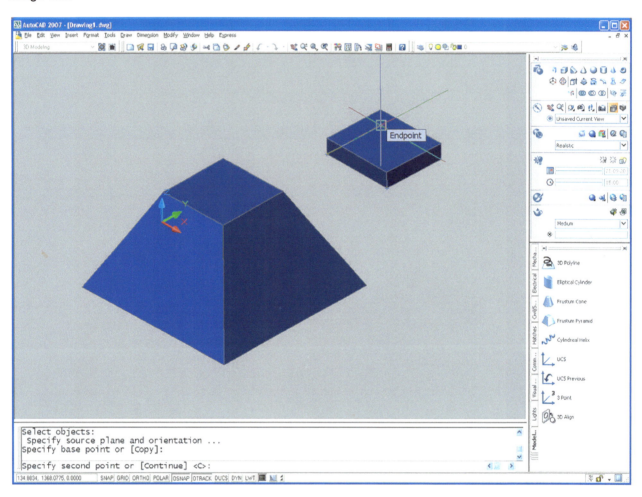

Specify third point on source plane as I've shown on image below.

Image 12.C

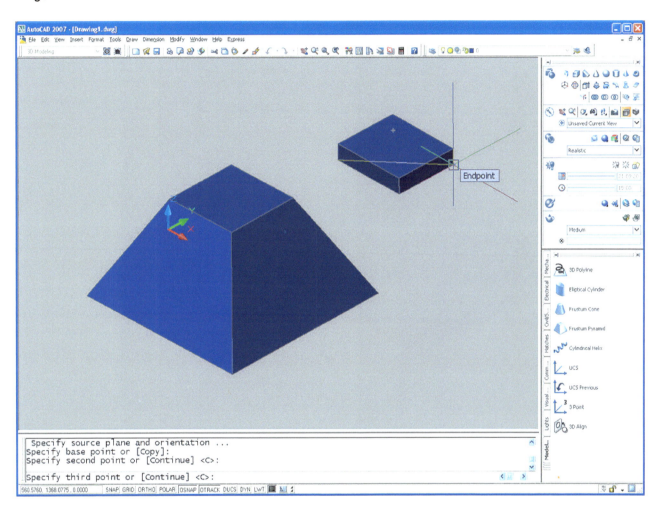

Align object to the new plane by specifying first destination point on the upper corner of the pyramid. See image below.

Image 12.D

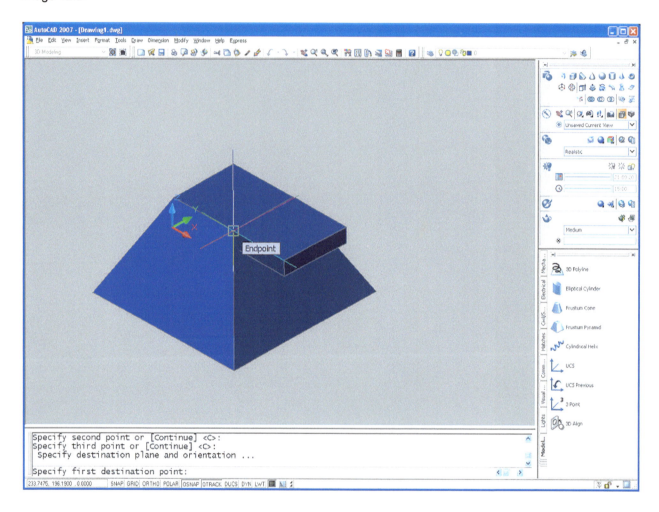

Specify second destination point on the upper corner of the pyramid. See image below.

Image 12.F

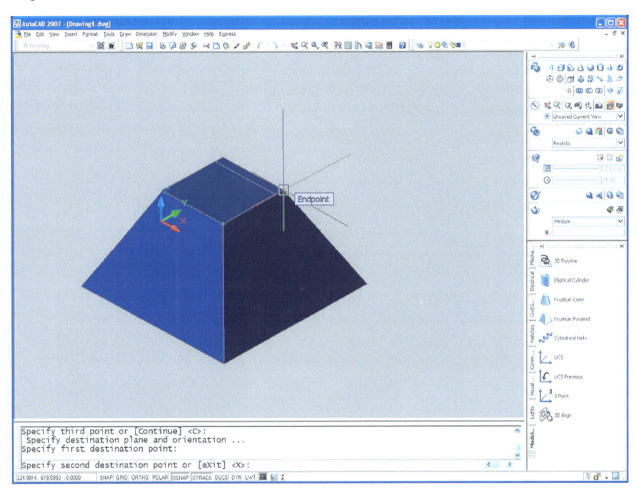

Specify third destination point perpendicular to the lowest side. See image below.

Image 12.G

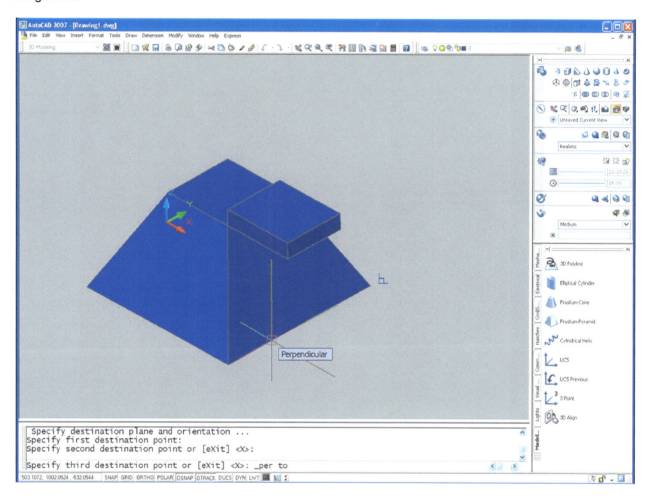

Final results. The 3D object is perfectly aligned with the frustum pyramid.

Image 12.H

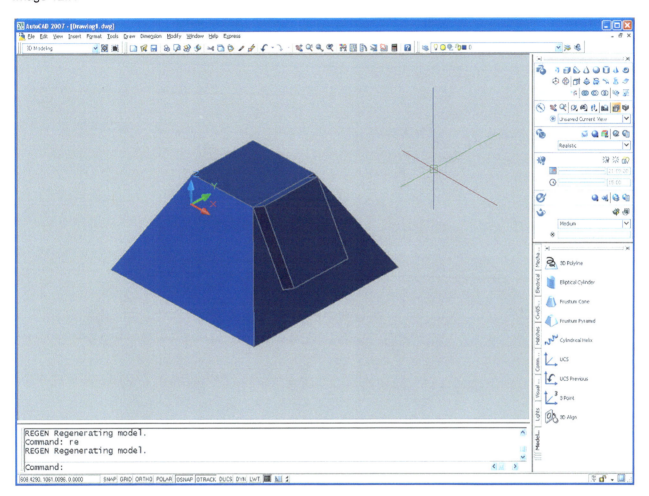

Section Plane

A long time missed feature in AutoCAD has finally arrived. It's the command SECTIONPLANE. You can make a cross section view of a house. I will explain you the easiest way to do this.

Type sectionplane in the command line, followed by enter.

Then chose <**Orthographic**> by typing O, followed by enter. Next you select **left** in the menu. You are done!

Image 14.A

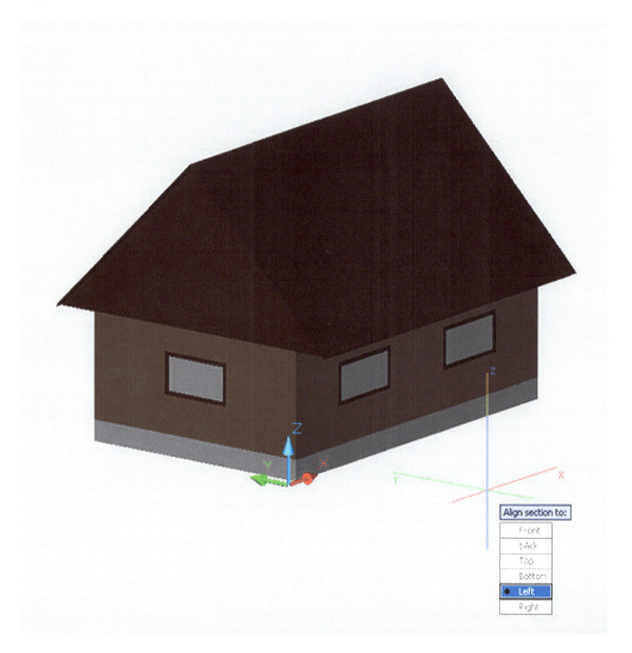

Final result, a cross section of the house.

Image 14.B

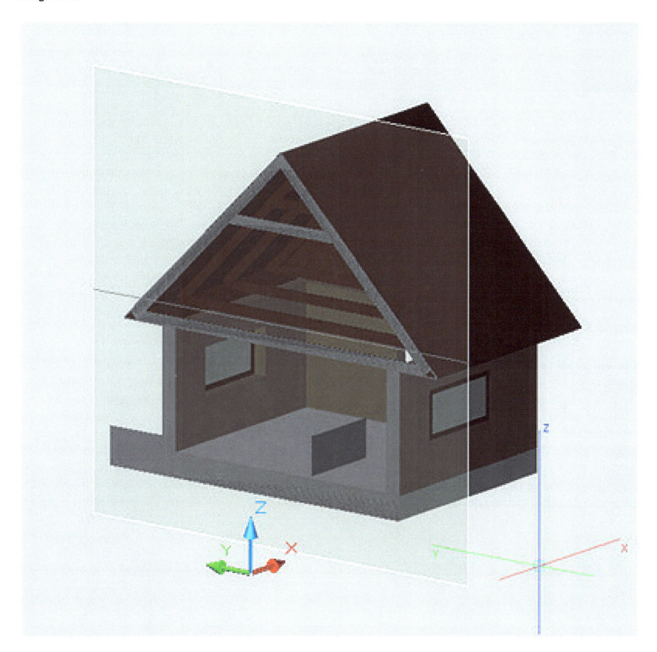

3D modeling and editing in AutoCAD can be done in a quick and easy manner.

Solve Problems in AutoCAD

Opening a AutoCAD Drawing

One common problem could be that you can't open a damaged drawing. Try the following techniques to solve the problem:

Find the autosave files (auto.sv$ by default) and rename them with a .DWG extension and try to open them. Use Windows search to find the autosave files, search with wildcard *.sv$. Rename the drawing's BAK (backup) file by changing its filename extension to .dwg and see if you can open that. Another thing you can do, that is to use the RECOVER command. Open a new drawing and choose File Drawing-> Utilities-> Recover. Choose the drawing from the dialog box and click OK. If you can open a drawing, but get an error message, then use the AUDIT command. You can find it right next to the RECOVER command on the File menu. AutoCAD tries to correct any errors. You can also open a new drawing with the "start from scratch option" to open a drawing with only a few settings. Finally, if you have parts of the drawing in another drawing, then there is the possibility to use WBLOCK to save all the objects in the drawing as a new drawing file.

AutoCAD is Crashing

You can overburden AutoCAD if your drawing has a big amount of data, containing more elements than the internal memory can handle. Perhaps you get the message; you are running low on memory. Most likely AutoCAD will crash at some point. Solve this by closing views and applications you are not using. You can purge the drawing twice, to reduce the amount of data in the DWG file. Ultimately you can add more memory to your computer. Another reason for crash can be a conflict between AutoCAD and the graphic card. I suggest you look for a software fix on Autodesk support pages. Often you find a solution from Autodesk. A conflict between Windows and AutoCAD can also cause a crash. Always maintain Windows, so it doesn't run with unnecessary drivers and files. If you can't detect and solve the error yourself, then contact your local AutoCAD support or search a solution on Autodesk's technical support web pages. Final advice: Keep AutoCAD updated.

www.ingramcontent.com/pod-product-compliance
Lightning Source LLC
Chambersburg PA
CBHW041422050326
40689CB00002B/617